ARTIFICIAL

INTELLIGENCE

Practical Guide To Obtain Competitive Advantage From
The Use Of Predictive Models And Enabling Technologies.

TOMMASO MAZZIOTTI

TABLE OF CONTENTS

Introduction

The idea of making machines and computers smarter started thousands of years ago, thanks to Western, Indian, Chinese, and Greek philosophers. These philosophers attempted to describe human thinking as a symbolic system.

Their efforts saw the slight light of day when their path of thinking led to the discovery of a machine based on the intellectual principle of mathematical reasoning in the 1940s. The machine in question was the programmable digital computer. The invention quickly inspired scientists all over the world and made them want to work harder to make intelligent machines become true.

One of those scientists was John McCarthy, who coined the word artificial intelligence during a conference he hosted at Dartmouth College in 1956. John McCarthy believed that an intelligent machine was possible to create if scientists would just come together and combine forces. He called a small group of scientists to come in and discuss the chances of them arising with an electric brain or, in other words, an intelligent machine.

After the conference, the participants concluded that it was possible to create a machine that rivaled human intelligence. The government liked the idea and financially sponsored the dream.

At the end of the 1960s, the scientist realized that the project was more ambitious than they initially thought because of hardware limitation. By then, the government was out of patience with them and withdrew financial support signaling years of difficulty for Artificial Intelligence (AI) research (because there was no funding).

In the 80s, the Government of Japan had a visionary initiative to support an expert system, which was further research towards AI. That inspired the governments of the U.S. and the U.K to reinstate their funding for AI research. The research got billions of dollars, but unfortunately, the governments ran out of patience waiting for the researchers to meet their objectives and they withdrew their funding once again.

Nowadays, artificial intelligence is becoming a part of our daily lives. AI is finding immense use in retail shops, cars, and health facilities.

All the greatness and success of artificial intelligence did not just come from nowhere; it was hinged on advanced development in an area called machine learning.

The Application We Know

The most believable application that we know of when it comes to artificial intelligence is that of the enemies inside video games. The problem is that this is not really intelligence. Or is it? The way that science defines intelligence is that "it is an entity that is capable of attaining new information and then using that information with past information to define current information." Therefore, the primary

7

problem with creating real intelligence is finding a way for machines to learn.

The reason why enemies inside video games are still called artificial intelligence is the mechanical nature of enemies in video games. The average person who plays a video game will look at a first-person shooter enemy as being intelligent in that the enemy will follow them. Therefore, if the player begins to hide, then the enemy will move closer while if the player is out in the open and shooting, the enemy will run for cover after firing a few bullets. This makes it seem like the enemy is actually thinking.

As you can see from the pseudocode above, if the line trace of where the enemy is pointing to does not equate to the player's collision but another object collision, then the enemy will move forward. This brings the enemy closer and creates the illusion that the enemy knows the player is hiding. However, if the player is targeting them and the line trace meets up with the player collision box, then the enemy will decide whether to fire at the player or hide behind a collision based on a randomized value. The line trace is the path of motion of the player.

The randomization creates the illusion that the enemy chooses whether they are going to duck underneath the cover or they're going to fire at the enemy. However, this is fake intelligence if we consider the fact that there is no past information being involved here. This is current information dealing with current decision-making. Additionally, the machine doesn't actually have any ability to learn about the character that they are going up against. This means that while the machine looks to be intelligent, there is no intelligence at playing. Instead, you have an instruction set pre-programmed by a thinking individual that tells the machine what to do given a certain case or a certain circumstance.

Now you might think that something like Amazon Echo or Google Home are hubs of real mechanical intelligence. The problem is that these machines are working in a very similar way to the enemies that we just covered.

Human speech is dictated by rules; you can think of them as the instruction set for how to speak the language. The important thing about rules is that if there are rules, a machine is most likely going to be able to follow those rules. Well, I won't get into the specifics of how recurrent neural networks work, but you can basically assume that the machine is simply analyzing and making probability statistics on what words likely fit together based on those rules. This is a very accurate way of determining which words you, as a person, are going to say whenever you use something like voice typing or when captions are made inside a video that has auto-translated your words.

Up until this point, we have not had many machines that are capable of learning and using that knowledge to further improve. However, we have just now entered the digital age of utilizing something called backpropagation.

Backpropagation is the center point of almost all machine learning algorithms that are currently at playing. A neural network is designed to take database input and perform actions on that information inside neurons that then produce an output. If the output is wrong, we then change what is occurring inside the neurons so that we try to get to a more optimized answer. The standard way of doing this is by taking the variables inside the neural network and creating sets of randomized variables to find the best-randomized variables. This is a very slow process and usually takes a very long time in order to perform. The new method is called backpropagation; what I just described to you is called forward propagation.

Instead of utilizing randomized variables and never knowing if you have reached the ultimate randomize combination, we use calculus and the outputs that the neural network has provided. The information is fed back into the neural network after the answer is performed incorrectly and the neural network takes the incorrect results as well as the numbers they used to get to those results and creates a combination that is more optimized as a result. Backpropagation represents the first form of machine learning that is actually intelligent. However, the vast majority of neural network applications, like Alexa and Siri, are not normally back-propagating networks in most situations. As time progresses, this actually might be changed but, backpropagation takes a lot of computing power that most devices simply don't have.

CHAPTER 1:

Introduction to Artificial Intelligence

Artificial intelligence is referred to as the science and engineering of intelligent machines. It is now considered as the most developed field of computer science because it allows machines to behave, think and make decisions like humans. Found on the principles of human-based skills, such as reasoning, solving problems and learning, AI includes programmed algorithms that can work and deliver output using its own intelligence.

Machine learning and artificial intelligence methodologies are combined to develop strong models and algorithms that are able to make correct predictions. Without human intervention, machines and computer programs are able to learn and make accurate decisions in order to deliver positive outcomes.

The aim of AI is to enhance the performance of computer functions that are linked to human knowledge, such as learning, problem solving and reasoning. Currently, researchers are working on different objectives of AI, including knowledge representation, natural language processing, learning, planning and realization.

Why Artificial Intelligence?

Based on the theories regarding computer science, psychology, biology, engineering and mathematics, artificial intelligence has made contributions in different fields, including health care, medical, robotics and self-driving machines.

Artificial intelligence methods and techniques are used to create software and devices that can solve real-world problems with a high level of accuracy. AI is intended to solve knowledge-intensive tasks, replicate human intelligence and create an intelligent connection of action and perception. With the help of AI, we can create personal virtual assistants, build robots to work in remote environments and unleash new possibilities for the development of technologies.

Disadvantages of AI

Although AI has provided long-term benefits and strong solutions, it has some disadvantages as well. No technology is perfectly developed and usually has initial problems that need to be addressed properly.

What's more, artificial intelligence is a costly solution because it requires lots of maintenance and routine upgrades. Moreover, the technology can never "think out of the box," as robots or machines will only perform the specific tasks that they are trained for. Humans are creative and can imagine new ideas, but with the rise of technology, people are getting dependent on smart devices and are slowly losing their mental capabilities.

AI machines are great performers and provide accurate results, but they do not have any kind of emotional attachments or feelings for humans. Sometimes this can be harmful to users as well.

Differences between Machine Learning and Artificial Intelligence

Machine learning is a subset of artificial intelligence and follows the symbolic rules, knowledge graphs, rules engines and models as defined in AI. When compared to AI, machine learning is dynamic and does not need human intervention to make the required changes as it is all about the acquisition of knowledge and skill. The aim of artificial intelligence is to increase the chance of success, whereas machine learning methods are more focused on achieving accuracy.

Artificial intelligence is also used to develop systems capable of mimicking humans in certain circumstances and will work to find the optimal solution. Models in AI are based on the decision-making approach, whereas the machine learning systems adopt new things from data. Also, machine learning involves the development of self-learning algorithms and leads to knowledge, and devices designed by using AI techniques have the capability to handle any task and operation with accurate results.

Natural language processing, expert systems, neural networks, robotics and fuzzy logic are the major subfields of artificial intelligence. Machine learning has the capability to automate analytical model building as it utilizes methods from operations research, physics, statistics and neural networks to find hidden insights in data without being explicitly programmed.

Subfields of Artificial Intelligence

Artificial intelligence is composed of multiple properties such as reasoning, learning, problem-solving, perception and linguistic intelligence. There are several ways to simulate human intelligence because some methods or models are more intelligent than others and AI is completely based on if-then statements, such as knowledge graphs, expert systems and rules engines. On the other hand, machine learning models are said to learn by experience and improve their performance without being explicitly programmed.

Here are some of the major subfields of artificial intelligence:

• *Neural networks*: Machine learning works similar to a human brain and is comprised of interconnected units. The information is then processed by responding to relaying information and external inputs between each unit. AI needs complete access to data for establishing connections to bring results from undefined data.

• *Computer vision:* It is focused on deep learning and pattern recognition approaches to recognize the information in a video or picture. With the help of AI models, machines are able to understand, analyze and capture images in real-time. Interpretation and evaluation of visuals can also be performed through computer vision techniques.

• *Natural language processing*: It is the ability of computers to understand, analyze, interpret and generate human language. As it is generally used in speech recognition models, humans can communicate with computers in their everyday language to perform specific tasks through natural language processing models. When an intelligence system performs any task as for the given instructions, the process of natural language is used for both input and output tasks. For example, spoken and written text.

• **Expert systems:** They are computer applications developed to solve complex problems at the level of human expertise and intelligence. Having high-performance, understandable, reliable, and highly responsive models, expert systems can easily instruct and assist humans in decision making. Moreover, the models are capable of advising, demonstrating and diagnosing different scenarios to interpret input and predict accurate results.

Characteristics of expert systems provide researchers the ability to develop computer applications for solving complex problems in a particular domain. These systems deliver high performance and better responsiveness. Additionally, expert systems are reliable, understandable and capable of deriving a solution. Predicting results, explaining, demonstrating and suggesting alternative options to a problem are now possible with expert system models. Major components of expert systems include a knowledge base, interface engine and user interface.

• **Deep Learning:** It is a subfield of machine learning and is based on the algorithms of artificial neural networks. This technique allows computers to perform activities in the same way humans do because it is inspired by the function and structure of the human brain. Deep learning technology is mainly being used in driverless cars and voice control applications in smartphones or computers. Besides, the computer model is intended to learn from classification tasks in the form of sound, text or image.

These models have a high level of accuracy and sometimes also exceed human-level performance because they are trained by using a large set of neural network architectures and labeled data. A deep learning algorithm will perform tasks repeatedly and learn from experience to improve the outcome. Neural networks have various deep layers that enable learning and allow machines to solve complex problems even with complex data set input.

Applications of deep learning include virtual assistants, translations, chatbots and service bots, vision for driverless delivery trucks, autonomous cars and drones, image colorization, facial recognition, medicine, personalized shopping, and entertainment.

Impact of AI in Everyday Life

Machine learning is a subfield of artificial intelligence and is based on the acquisition of knowledge. Through AI models and algorithms, we can make intelligent computer systems that can understand human language and respond accordingly. This technology is being implemented in hospitals to keep patients safer and make their recovery faster. Moreover, AI can now be found in advanced security systems and cameras through which finding people and things in real-time has now been made possible.

Artificial intelligence has impacted our lives on a daily basis at every level. Smartphones and digital devices are updated with the latest features, such as built-in assistants Alexa and Siri. Also, the finance industry and other companies heavily rely on artificial intelligence models for customer service, investments, fraud protection and chatbots. Moreover, spam filters in Gmail inbox are powered with AI to avoid fake emails.

CHAPTER 2:

The Benefits and Disadvantages of AI

Many different parts come with this kind of technology, but not everyone is on board with it, and there are some disadvantages that we need to discuss as well. Both the benefits and the disadvantages are important to help us determine where artificial intelligence should go in the future and to know whether it is the right option for us to use or not.

In addition to discussing a bit about its benefits and the negatives, we also need to look into some of the ethical questions that come in. Many times, we get excited about all the different things this technology can do for us that we do not think about what could go wrong. Looking into how artificial intelligence can be manipulated or used wrongly and how to make sure that the program does not show any bias from its programmer can determine how we can handle the changing artificial learning algorithms in the future.

As we can already see, many things come into using artificial intelligence, and it is not always as easy to focus on as we may think. This is not necessarily a bad thing, but we must not just jump in and go all in without any thoughts. So, let us dive in and explore the benefits, the disadvantages, and the ethics that come with artificial intelligence.

The Benefits of Artificial Intelligence

As we have stated throughout this guidebook, working with artificial intelligence comes with a lot of benefits. There are so many different industries that use this technology, as well as so many different ways it can be utilized. With that in mind, we have to take a look at some of the various reasons why individuals, especially companies, would want to use this kind of technology to help them out.

These machines reduce error rates. When you use a machine that has artificial intelligence on it, we will see that the risk of error is lower compared to the work that humans do. This is one of the biggest advantages because it can save some industries millions of dollars. With the use of the information that is already in artificial intelligence, along with some of the algorithms with it, the decisions for a company can be made quickly. The results are not only fast and easy, but the accuracy can be a lifesaver to a lot of different companies.

Artificial intelligence is also fast and results in some quick actions, much faster than what we see with what a human or even a team of humans can do. Artificial intelligence can make decisions and work quickly. The brain of the machine, which is integrated with artificial intelligence, takes actions so quickly that it can help to provide you with results in no time at all.

It also helps out in daily work. Are you already using Google Assistant? Do you work with Alexa and some of the other voice-activated assistants daily? Do you have a Smart Home and you have to speak to it to get things set at the way that you want? If any of these sound familiar to you, then you can already see how artificial intelligence can help you out in your daily work.

Working without brakes is another benefit that you get with AI. As a regular person, we need to take a break after we do so much work. We all get tired; our brains are not designed to work 24/7 all the time without any breaks. We need time away from work, a break, and some time to relax and do what we want and what we enjoy rather than working all of the time.

This is normal for most of us to deal with, but it can slow down work and productivity. When we work with an AI machine, we see that it does not get tired and it can work without all of the breaks. For many businesses, this can be good news. The machines that are integrated with artificial intelligence can work for a much longer duration of time at high speed and a high amount of accuracy at the same time.

Artificial intelligence machines are better at assisting than humans. These kinds of assistants can make much better decisions without adding in the emotions and biases we see with humans. Sometimes, these emotions and biases are good for us and can help with decisions, but often, they get in the way and they will cause us to make poor decisions along the way. This becomes less of a problem when we work with artificial intelligence.

Since the artificial intelligence machine does not have to work with these emotions, they can work efficiently without having any personal issues in the process. Besides, when we look at how this technology is used as a chatbot, we see that they are designed to chat about the problems that will help a human find their solution, and nothing else, so the emotions are kept to a minimum.

For the most part, these machines can reach much further than we would be able to do on our own. Due to a lot of the risk that comes with it, there are some places, and sometimes some circumstances, where humans cannot reach. Think about something like a fire, an important location for the military, and even some projects that take place out in space. When these kinds of situations occur, rather than taking on too much risk along the way, a robot—one that has been programmed with artificial intelligence—would be able to complete the task and it can be done without any human interaction. Such a machine, if it is done and programmed correctly, can do the work and reach places where humans are more limited.

Another benefit is **the utility there is for society.** We mentioned a bit earlier about the chatbots. These are helpful because they can listen to a voice command, then it will go through and translate it for someone who does not know that particular language but who would still like to talk.

This is just one example of how artificial intelligence can help out the society. Another one is with the idea of a self-driving car, which you can use to reach the location that you want, with better road safety and no crashes in the process.

And finally, we can look at how the idea of artificial intelligence can benefit us with some of the possible future innovations. Right now, one example of using this kind of technology is with Google AI, which is already looking at how it can be implemented in Biosciences and Healthcare. Recently, you may have heard about how this process will be able to detect things like diabetes by determining the retina depth. And if it is used properly, it can find more common diseases in humans and help us to get more benefits for our health in the process.

The Disadvantages of Artificial Intelligence

While artificial intelligence has a lot of benefits, and it seems like more and more people and businesses are coming on board with this kind of technology and trying to use it for their needs, some disadvantages come with this process as well. It is not always as positive as you may think, and while a lot of companies decide to use it for their needs and to help them grow and provide better customer service for their customers, there are some times when it is not the best decision for you.

What are these disadvantages? And how can you tell whether using artificial intelligence is the right option for you? Below are some of the disadvantages that you can watch out for, and at least consider, when it comes to the growth of artificial intelligence and using AI in your business.

Artificial intelligence can be too expensive. One of the biggest problems and one of the main reasons why people choose not to use this in their business is that constructing a system or a machine that uses this technology can be expensive. Think about how much work needs to be done in this process to make things work and how much it will cost to have enough power, to make the algorithm, to sort through the data, and more. For some big businesses, this cost makes sense and can save them money. But for some of the smaller companies, the cost is just going to be too big and they will forgo using this process.

Because AI-integrated machines are very complex, they cost more to maintain and use. In addition to this, they also cost a lot to keep the system up and running as well as the repair. Artificial intelligence is relatively new right now, which means that these machines, even though they may be relatively new, have to be updated constantly with the changing technology.

Instead of having emotions to help guide it, artificial intelligence relies on coding and programming. Deciding in some circumstances does not work with these programs, and sometimes, it is based on emotions. You will not be able to do this the right way with artificial intelligence, and that can mean that some decisions are not made correctly.

The artificial intelligence machine does not have any continuous self-development. A lot of times, humans learn a lot from the time they are children up until they are adults and so on. This is natural with humans and it means that they can learn and self-develop at the same time from the experiences that they had in the past. But this is not something that we see with artificial intelligence; it does not have any experience, really, but it will be based on the programming it has been given. The machine only has a chance to "learn" something new if we take the time to update the program.

The AI machine does not have any innovation by itself. As we take a look at humans, we can see throughout the years that they have always been creative. This is a gift that we have been given by nature, and all of us have different levels of creativity. Some of us are creative with writing, some with drawing, some with music, some with coding, and so on. Each of us has a different type of creativity, but as a whole, humans are born with some kind of creativity, and this is the basis of our developing world right now.

But think about a machine. Does that machine can do something brand new and be creative on its own without the programmer? Artificial intelligence, at least now, has not been built to handle this kind of process. It can help us in a lot of different ways. It can be useful for businesses and customers in many cases. But for now, at least, it cannot handle anything like creativity and innovation all on its own.

The last disadvantage would be the idea of human replacement. The machine that uses artificial intelligence can indeed help us out in many ways and sometimes do things that are not within reach of us as humans. But it can never completely replace what a human can do.

CHAPTER 3:

How Artificial Intelligence Is
Changing Many Industries

Artificial Intelligence is leading the Fourth Industrial Revolution with its growing influence on everyday consumer products. AI has revamped the manufacturing, retail, and finance industries with new products, processes, and capabilities. Some of the most significant breakthroughs in physics and healthcare are also credited to AI. In this era of technological advancements as we move towards a future depicted in science fiction, AI has become an essential part of our world. Artificial Intelligence has exploded in recent years, thanks to the massive amount of online data we generate every day and the never seen before powerful computers. The business leaders and innovators are chasing the promise of AI to gain a competitive advantage while saving up on costs and time. From optimizing the delivery route to management of a global supply chain, AI is helping companies of all sizes across the industries to improve their bottom line with enhanced productivity. Companies are able to design, produce, and deliver superior products and services while cutting back on their expenses. Isn't that every entrepreneur's dream come true?!?!

Journalism Industry

Is a bit surprising right, reports being replaced by computers? It's not easy to process how something as subjective and emotionally driven as journalism can be done by machines. But, about a third of content published by the "Bloomberg News" is currently using some form of Artificial Intelligence. Bloomberg is using a system called "Cyborg" that is designed to assist reporters in writing thousands of news articles pertaining to the company's earnings report every quester. As soon as financial data is available to the program, it dissects the report and generates a news story with the most pertinent facts and figures. Poles apart from most business reporters who ascertain this type of reporting as boring and tiresome, Cyborg works accurately and without fatigue. Bloomberg is rivaled by Reuters in the field of high-speed business financial journalism, and with the help of Cyborg, Bloomberg is slated to win big. The newest player in the race of financial information is Hedge Funds, who are already using AI to provide their customers with update facts and figures.

There are, of course, certain limitations to machine-generated news articles. For instance, companies that choose to 'adjust' their net earnings or profit figures in an effort to portray a greener future than their number warrants can easily bypass the AI in producing a more favorable and biased article. Although kudos to Bloomberg, who is making efforts to prepare Cyborg to not be duped by such misleading tactics. Remember, Artificial Intelligence is only able to assist human reporters. Journalists are still required to do the legwork, draft multiple versions of a story with text for a variety of outcomes and feed all that data into the machine, which then churns out new articles. For example, news articles pertaining to a weather event, football game, and yes, even an earnings statement require human reporters to get the groundwork done in the front end of the system.

Healthcare Industry

With the increasing availability of healthcare data, AI has brought on a paradigm shift to healthcare. The primary focus of Artificial Intelligence in the healthcare industry is the analysis of relationships between patient outcomes and the treatment or prevention technique used. AI programs have successfully been developed for patient diagnostics, treatment protocol generation, drug development, as well as patient monitoring and care. The powerful AI techniques can sift through a massive amount of clinical data and help unlock clinically relevant information to assist in decision making.

In 1965, Artificial Intelligence researcher Edward Feigenbaum and geneticist Joshua Lederberg, developed the first major application of heuristic programming for chemical analysis called DENDRAL. This was the first-ever rule-based system that had real-world applications. Molecular structure illustration has been a substantive problem in organic chemistry since the chemical and physical properties of a compound are determined not just by the constituent atoms but by their geometric arrangement. Mass spectrometry could provide information about the constituent atoms but it is insensitive to the geometry of the atoms. The ability of DENDRAL to hypothesize the molecular structure of a compound rivaled the performance of chemistry experts.

Some medical specialties with increasing AI research and use are:

Radiology – The ability of AI to interpret imaging results supplements clinicians' ability to detect changes in an image that can easily be missed by the human eye. An AI algorithm recently created at Stanford University can detect specific sites in the lungs of the pneumonia patients.

Electronic Health Records – The need for digital health records to optimize the information spread and access requires fast and accurate logging of all health-related data in the systems. A human is prone to errors and may be affected by cognitive overload and burnout. This process has been successfully automated by AI. The use of Predictive models on the electronic health records data allowed the prediction of individualized treatment response with 70-72% accuracy at baseline.

Imaging – Ongoing AI research is helping doctors in evaluating the outcome of corrective jaw surgery as well as in assessing the cleft palate therapy to predict facial attractiveness.

Here are some of the most potent Artificial Intelligence advancements in healthcare:

AI-assisted robotic surgery – The biggest draw of robot-assisted surgery is that they do not require large incisions and are considered minimally invasive with low post-op recovery time. Robots are capable of analyzing data from pre-op patient medical records and subsequently guiding the surgeon's instruments during surgery. These robot-assisted surgeries have reported up to a 21% reduction in patients' hospital stays. Robots can also use data from past surgeries and use AI to inform the surgeon about any new possible techniques. The most advanced surgical robot, "Da Vinci," allows surgeons to carry out complex surgical procedures with higher accuracy and greater control than the conventional methods.

Supplement clinical diagnosis – Although the use of AI in diagnostics is still under the radar, a lot of successful use cases have already been reported. An algorithm created at Stanford University is capable of detecting skin cancer with similar competencies as that of a skilled dermatologist. An AI software program in Denmark was used to eavesdrop on emergency phone calls made to human dispatchers. The underlying algorithm analyzed the tone and words of the caller as well as the background noise to detect cases of a heart attack. The AI program had a 93% success rate, which was 20% higher than the human counterparts.

Virtual Nursing Assistants – The virtual nurses are available 24/7 without fatigue and lapse in judgment. They provide constant patient monitoring and directions for the most effective care while answering all of the patient's questions quickly and efficiently. An increase in regular communication between patients and their care providers can be credited to virtual nursing applications. This prevents unnecessary hospital visits and readmission. The virtual nurse assistant at Care

Angel can already provide wellness checks through Artificial Intelligence and voice.

Finance or Banking Industry

The tech giants tend to hog most of the limelight when it comes to cutting edge technological advancements. But the financial sector, including the stodgy banking incumbents, are showing increasing interest and signs of adoption of Artificial Intelligence. The banking or finance industry has a profound impact on virtually all consumers and businesses with a direct effect on the country's economy, so seeking insight and keeping up to date with the convergence of financial technology and Artificial Intelligence is critical for every business. The banking industry is putting its money on Artificial Intelligence based solutions to address a lot of traditional banking problems such as providing quality customer service to their millions of customers, fraud prevention, mobile technology, and data security, among others.

Here are some popular Artificial Intelligence-based trends in banking:

In the 1960s, in an effort to coordinate the bookings made by travel agents across the US, the travel industry pioneered large scale industrial computing, with the arrival of computer-based airline booking systems. Most travel companies are collecting data from users, and with the right Artificial Intelligence tools, they are able to provide customers with relevant future travel programs based on their past searches. The use of Artificial Intelligence pricing tools that can autonomously adjust flight prices depending on the market demand, weather, and other determining factors is helping airlines optimize their business.

When prospective travelers browse, shop, book, fly or even change their travel plans, companies collect this data, which is analyzed by Artificial Intelligence powered solutions to gather actionable insights and custom tailor their services to the customer's needs. The competition in the travel industry is fierce, with the savvy travelers always comparing and looking for prices of flights, hotels, buses, trains, and car rentals to get the best out of their buck. Artificial Intelligence has immense potential to alter the travel experience with personalized services and efficient travel experience.

Transportation Industry

The transportation industry is highly susceptible to two problems arising from human errors, traffic, and accidents. These problems are too difficult to model owing to their inherently unpredictable nature, but can be easily overcome with the use of Artificial Intelligence-powered tools that can analyze observed data and make or predict the appropriate decisions. The challenge of increasing travel demand, safety concerns, CO_2 emissions, and environmental degradation can be met with the power of artificial intelligence. From Artificial Neural Networks to Bee colony optimization, a whole lot of artificial intelligence techniques are being employed to make the transportation industry efficient and effective. To obtain significant relief from traffic congestion while making travel time more reliable for the population, transport authorities are experimenting with a variety of AI-based solutions. With the potential application of artificial intelligence for enhanced road infrastructure and assistance for drivers, the transportation industry is focused on accomplishing a more reliable transport system, which will have limited to no effect on the environment while being cost-effective.

 It is an uphill battle to fully understand the relationships between the characteristics of various transportation systems using traditional methods. Artificial intelligence is here once again to offer the panacea by transforming the traffic sensors on the road into a smart agent that can potentially detect accidents and predict future traffic conditions. Rapid development has been observed in the area of Intelligent Transport Systems (ITS), which are targeted to alleviate traffic congestion and improve the driving experience by utilizing multiple technologies and communication systems. They are capable of collecting and storing data that can be easily integrated with machine learning technology. To increase the efficiency of police patrol and keeping the citizens of safe collection of crime data is critical and can be achieved with the right AI-powered tools. Artificial intelligence can also simplify the transportation planning of the road freight transport system by providing accurate prediction methods to forecast its volume.

Education Industry

The emergence of artificial intelligence and machine learning technology is set to alter and revitalize education tools and institutions while revamping the future of education. Multiple changes can be anticipated to a teacher's job as well as to educational best practices with the increasing use of AI-powered tools in education, but the critical presence of teachers will remain irreplaceable. With the increasing use of artificial intelligence for education, the academic world will become even more convenient and personalized. The way people learn is changing at a rapid pace; educational materials are easily accessible to computers and smart devices. The traditional method of being in the classroom to obtain an education is being challenged by the convenience of at-home Internet connection on students' computers. AI is also bringing convenience to the indicators and academic institutions by cutting down the time spent on administrative tasks that can easily be automated using artificial intelligence.

CHAPTER 4:

How Artificial Intelligence Is Changing Business Processes

Business process, as we know, is changing, thanks to the power of artificial intelligence. The rate at which AI is changing how business is processing information is dizzying. More organizations are taking advantage of the promises of artificial intelligence. The difference AI is making in such

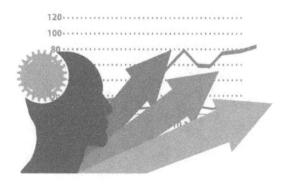

organizations is clear.

Companies are increasing their levels of efficiency to never seen before standards using AI tools. Operations that were taking days to complete are now over in hours or less. Some AI tools can achieve speed without losing quality. Workers are getting much-needed support from AI tools leading to better outcomes.

The more the AI tools get incorporated into business processes, the more innovations are increasing. Modifications of AI tools are occurring as their use is growing in businesses. The workforce is getting more creative to survive the onslaught by machines. They are also getting more time to create, as AI devices are taking over mundane tasks.

Artificial intelligence has brought the facet of convenience to business processes. Procedures previously taking hours to complete can now be finished in comparatively shorter periods, sometimes with the click of a button. Industries based on this factor brought in by AI are blossoming, for example, completely e-commerce based businesses.

Businesses are now able to take advantage of growth opportunities that were not available before the advent of AI. Brick and mortar stores can run e-commerce shops in tandem. Businesses can reach customers that were previously unavailable to them at a minimal cost. The range of products companies can offer customers are also growing.

AI is converting manual business processes into automated procedures. Companies are using this opportunity to stay ahead of the competition as automation is allowing them to reach more customers in shorter periods. Faster processing is attracting more clients to businesses. Automation is also lowering business costs. Businesses are now able to incorporate segmentation into their internal and external processes. The effect on marketing is companies having the ability to personalize product offerings. The use of beacons as a way of optimizing sales promotions is becoming more common among business marketing strategies.

Businesses are adding value to products and services using AI-backed tools. Some products previously unavailable in digital forms are now in production in e-formats thanks to AI-driven possibilities.

AI is changing business processes including, customer acquisition, new customer service types, personal assistants in businesses, marketing research, human resource and hiring, and the sales process. The extent to which the methods are changing is proportional to the investment businesses are putting in concerning AI-backed tools.

How Artificial Intelligence Is Changing Marketing Research

Historically, marketing research involves sending the human workforce to chosen areas where they would ask questions to a predetermined sample population. The answers would give a glance at the opinion of the market towards a product or service. Data would come from the answers, and analysis would generate a conclusion. The whole process was tedious and would take months, even years, to conclude. The cost implication of the process was high in terms of money and time. The possibility of a research result, being redundant by the time it was submitted, was a possible reality. Artificial intelligence is changing marketing research by erasing some of the challenges previously experienced within the industry. Marketing research companies can now carry out work conveniently and can, therefore, interact with larger populations. The result is higher levels of accuracy. The convenience is breaking down barriers that had fewer people willing to take part in surveys. For the research done remotely, the privacy factor associated is giving researchers a larger pool of individuals willing to share their opinions on issues. The timing of responses is also now convenient with respondents choosing appropriate times of answering surveys.

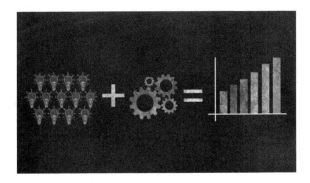

Artificial intelligence is giving marketing research companies opportunities to expand their reach of possible respondents. Through AI, market research is now possible on a global scale. Geographical barriers are a thing of the past for market research companies that are embracing the use of AI in their research processes. AI is tackling barriers like cultures that were a hindrance to marketing research. Examples include those that inhibit part of the population from giving their opinions on varied issues. AI is allowing individuals to share their views without necessarily revealing who they are, which is allowing more people to comment.

With AI, marketing research companies can segment their target population at a faster rate. At the click of a button, a company can determine the boundaries of the sample population. The limits to be defined can include geography, age, sex, gender, religion, and work. The potential of targeting accuracy is more with AI-backed marketing research tools. Targeting with AI gives results that are a better reflection of reality.

Marketing research companies working on a global scale can determine the appropriate timing of the process for region. The result may be an increase in the number of respondents for the survey that is carried out. Artificial intelligence is allowing marketing research companies to carry out their processes online. The benefits of online platforms are numerous, including the opportunity for marketing research companies to tweak surveys as results are coming in. Marketing research companies can add or reduce the scope of their research as respondents are acting. There are marketing research companies that are creating applications that send out surveys as needed. A notification would pop up on the devices of potential respondents, giving them a chance to share their opinions conveniently. Online research is allowing companies to see results in real-time. The advent of AI in marketing research has considerably reduced the turnaround time for results. Marketing research companies can see the results as they are trickling in from respondents. The speed is allowing for versatility with marketing research companies carrying out multiple types of research concurrently. The companies can serve many customers while using their resources efficiently. Businesses looking for quick turnaround times from market research companies are at an advantage. The quick turnaround time is proving beneficial to organizations as they can react to the market faster. Businesses can use AI marketing research as a tool to keep abreast of market changes.

How Artificial Intelligence is Changing Human Resources and Hiring

Human resources is an industry as old as the advent of businesses. The focus of human resources is the people element of an organization. The people in a business can cause an organization to succeed or fail, which explains the importance of the human resources industry. The success of the human resource department directly reflects in the performance of a business. The industry should, therefore, keep abreast of developments, which allow them to attract the best people for a business. A workforce can be the competitive edge for an organization. In many parts of the world, unemployment is rising. The human resources department of most organizations is receiving tons of resumes from applicants whenever they advertise for opportunities. Sifting through the documentation was a nightmare in yesteryears. The advent of AI use in human resources is automating this process. The availability of AI software to sift through resumes sent by applicants is reducing the administrative workload for human resources departments. AI is allowing the human resources industry to focus on the central tasks of interviewing the right applicants for vacant positions. AI resume processing is also allowing human resources to sift through more resumes than ever before.

AI is making tremendous changes within the human resources industry with online platforms budding based on this industry. Platforms like LinkedIn are allowing recruiters to reach potential team players via non-traditional methods. It is not uncommon to find human resource departments sifting through the social media platforms of applicants for a glance of who applicants are. The job marketplace is expecting potential workers to have a presence on these platforms. Some vacancies are filling based on the profiles on these platforms. Connections among the workforce in these platforms are leading to opportunities in organizations.

Human resources, being a competitive edge in the marketplace, have AI to thank for providing opportunities for companies to outsource tasks as needed. Smaller companies can get vital tasks sorted without the process of hiring an individual permanently. Many companies are opting to use freelancers for delegable tasks. AI, in this way, has led to the growth of the freelance industry spanning a variety of jobs. Organizations can, through freelancing, attract highly skilled individuals for required periods whom they would ordinarily be unable to afford. The arrangement offers companies opportunities to leverage the available global workforce to minimize hiring costs.

How Artificial Intelligence Is Changing the Sales Process

Artificial intelligence is changing how organizations are approaching the sales process. Tools backed by AI are now a staple of the business sales process. The Customer Relationship Management (CRM) tool is an AI-backed software that organizations are incorporating to make their sales process more effective. The benefits of these tools include faster responses and better follow up to sales leads. Teams can interact remotely, making better decisions for organizations.

Companies are finding it easier to follow up with their sales personnel on the ground using the software. Organizations can access sales data on a real-time basis allowing faster reactions to the market dynamics. Organizations can now carry out a complete sales process online, for example, through e-commerce stores. Some businesses are completely online while others are taking advantage of the opportunities, and adding the e-commerce component to their brick and mortar stores. The effect is that organizations can reach more customers at minimal cost, which translates to higher operational efficiency for businesses. The advent of AI in the online space is allowing for the rise of new sales promotional methods like the use of online bidding. Companies can access the global market using online platforms, therefore, increasing their potential market share.

Artificial intelligence in the sales process is giving rise to the use of applications (abbreviated as apps) in promoting sales. Many companies now have apps that potential clients can download onto their devices through which they can access varied services, including making orders. Such applications can give companies access to information on potential clients that they would have no other way of getting. With the data, companies can personalize the sales process to an individual level, which gives organizations greater accuracy of sales impact.

Businesses can use the data as a competitive edge in the marketplace because they create products that will resonate with their potential clients. For businesses to succeed, they must make a profit enough to sustain the enterprise. Some companies allow for credit, whose basis is the belief that the buyer will be able to afford the payments in the future. Artificial Intelligence is providing tools for businesses to analyze, in advance, whether an individual can pay for their services or products in the future through their use in the credit report systems. Companies can use these systems to take calculated risks while taking advantage of opportunities.

CHAPTER 5:

Chatbots and How They Will Change Communication

Getting Rid of Easy Problems

A lot of time in the customer service area is simply wasted on directing customers towards the area of a website or landmass or towards a product they can't find. It's usually due to a layout issue of that area they are looking at that causes this problem.

Artificial intelligence can pick up on keywords like "can you help me find" and then find the product page or area they are trying to find. This is a very simple interaction that takes time from the customer service and that can easily be handled by artificial intelligence. A customer simply logs in to a website, starts searching around it, and then reads about a product that sounds awesome, but they can't find it. That's when they usually reach out to customer service to help them find it. While you are fixing common issues so that it doesn't happen again, you can have artificial intelligence do the redirecting across all your websites and project pages so that the issue is immediately resolved, and this can be logged into a database of queries.

Simple Changes with Billing

In companies like Comcast, Electrical, AT&t, and other companies that require a subscription on a monthly basis, a user is likely going to need to change information about their billing arrangements. Simple billing changes would be of address where the individual can't find the location to do that or changing the bank account that is associated to. These simple changes can be handled by artificial intelligence because they happen in a predictable manner.

Customer service answers the phone and unless there is a specific template set up, a lot of the time the agent winds up wasting is time figuring out the wants of the customer. Once they can find out the wants of the customer, they then spend time figuring out how to do it for the customer themselves. Normally, this interaction takes anywhere from 10 to 20 minutes while putting an additional wait time for the customer at around 10 to 20 minutes. By using artificial intelligence, they can essentially save around half an hour for phone call.

Providing Remedies to Complaints

Another portion of the time that is wasted on customer service is customer complaints. Let me use a Comcast example of how to find out whether your internet is currently down or not. If you were to rewind by around 5 years and called Comcast to see if your internet in the area was down, you would call the customer service line and ask why your internet is not working. If you're a little bit tech savvy, you would have done the rudimentary steps beforehand. However, most people simply say that their internet is not working, and so half an hour of their time would be wasted on diagnosing the issue.

I don't think I have to inform you that waiting an hour to just find out that you have an internet shortage in the area is somewhat frustrating and definitely agitating. Now, if you call Comcast, they have artificial intelligence handling the problem. The artificial intelligence takes your phone number and compares it to the billing arrangements that are attached to that phone number. They then check the address of where you're located to a database that has a listing of current outages as well as repair times. The artificial intelligence then informs you that you have an internet outage in your area and gives you a specific time at which the problem will be solved. A call that was previously taking an hour per customer was reduced to artificial intelligence providing an answer in as little as 10 minutes from when you first make the call to customer service. When you are dealing with millions of customers, going from 60 minutes to 10 minutes drastically changes the amount of time available.

Noting Easy Answers that Don't Work

As I alluded to before, sometimes simple answers don't work and need to be refined. The problem is usually that the customer is not adequately providing answers to the artificial intelligence and the solution to such problem is to refine the question that you're asking. It's as simple as an interview. You will get as good information as you want, providing that you have questions that specifically target that information.

Therefore, if someone says, "I can't find the about page" and you link them to the about page through artificial intelligence, but it doesn't actually have the mission statement that they were looking for, you have a dissatisfied customer and an algorithm that gave them the wrong answer according to their opinion. At this point, the algorithm should lead the user to an actual customer representative to help them and then note that what they were really looking for wasn't on the about page. Then you go into artificial intelligence and create a condition where the artificial intelligence asks the user if they are looking for the mission statement. Now the artificial intelligence can handle all further customers looking for just the mission statement of your company because the customer usually thinks all mission statements are in the about page.

Personalized Attention

A lot of customer service time is wasted because they are trying to gather information on the customer that they are talking to. They are trying to find what the original problem was and being introduced to a stranger, the customer service representative has no idea what they really want. By having an artificial intelligence begin asking questions, the customer service representative can move past figuring out what the customer wants or, at the very least, they are able to shorten the discussion to an incredibly small length so that they can get to the solution much faster than they would have.

Reduce Customer Service Workloads

Get Rid of Basic Problems

As I said, most customer services problems lie in solving basic, common issues. If a customer is looking in laundry products for a scent ball that they can throw into the laundry basket, but they are not finding it because you put it in the beauty products section, they will likely contact customer service to try to find it.

This wastes an extremely high amount of time on customer service because if one customer is going to ask it then you likely have a hundred more customers that are going to try to ask it and they will ask it in 10 different ways. This means customer service agents are just trying to find products for a customer and unless that customer is particularly website or store savvy, they are not going to be able to find it without the customer service agent breaking it down into English language that elementary students could understand.

That isn't to say that customers are dumb, it's just that sometimes things like accents and the way you say things will interfere with the message that's coming across. Artificial intelligence can be set up to handle general requests for products, so if they are looking for a specific type of product then the artificial intelligence is able to provide them with a link to where they can find that product or a description of different places they could find that on your website. This ultimately saves time for both the customer and the customer service agent.

Get Rid of Redirection Issues

Sometimes you have customers that want to do more than what's available on the website itself. For instance, 90% of the reason why a person looks at an about page is that they are looking to do more than the basic customer service and are looking to do business to business service. These are companies that are trying to find out what type of company you are and what type of products you will likely provide in the future along with what morals you hold your company to.

The problem is that most of these types of individuals do the same thing but in different ways. For instance, one customer might look at an about page and then travel off site to look at LinkedIn pages of employees working there. Another customer might look at the affiliated links to find out where the connections to your company are and how big of a reach you have. In both situations, the customer is trying to figure out who you are as a business and artificial intelligence can pick up on that. These can be handled in many different ways, such as flagging them in a database so that you know that this particular customer is doing this or you could start up a chat in artificial intelligence and ask if the customer is interested in investing in the business. This really is an opinion-based approach because while one could just be cool knowledge to have, the other could be seen as an intrusive way of business.

Specialized Issues Are Faster

Sometimes websites don't work the way that we want them to do and so when a customer tries to reach out to customer service to resolve the issue, they used to have to wait for customer service to be done with all the basic stuff and all the redirecting. Artificial intelligence can find out information the customer wants to provide and usually, it can pick up on things like a bug or "this didn't go the way it was supposed to." These would be based on the words in the sentence, such as "I think you have a bug in the website," "something went wrong when I try to do this," or such similar phrasing and this can be redirected to a technical support line. This would allow developers to react to situations more quickly than if the user had gone through a customer service representative and then customer service representative figures out that there was a bug and that the customer was just wasting the time of the customer service agent simply because the customer can't connect to anyone else.

Reduced Time Spent as a Result

Every phone call that is wasted on basic problems, redirecting, or issuing bug reports is a phone call that costs money. Customer service representatives often work by the hour, which means that you are paying them to solve your customer's problems as fast as possible. By getting rid of the majority of the basic problems and issues that your website has by turning this over to a Chatbots system, you alternatively save how much time the customer service agency uses in day-to-day problem-solving. While you are likely not going to reduce the amount of time that the customer service area is open, customers who would come back and tie up the lines the next day because customer service agents were offline can now be handled by artificial intelligence if they have a problem while customer service agents are not available. This saves even more time because customers who have to call the next day will cause customers that are calling that day to call the next day and so the issue becomes a compounded algorithmic catastrophe that whines up wasting a lot of time.

CHAPTER 6:

How Artificial Intelligence Is Changing the Job Market

All Jobs Will Be Replaced

Let's cut to the chase because every time that this topic comes up, it's really associated with the job that's being replaced. The problem with this topic is that people see the short-term result of what a specific technology will do. The truth of the matter is that all of the jobs in current existence will be replaced, given enough time. It is extremely easy to define and put into place machines for cooking hamburgers. The fact that we refrigerate hamburgers that are pre-made proves this point. Machines can already do most of the basic work that we need them to do.

It is not difficult to automate something, but what is difficult is choosing what needs to be automated. If you have ever talked to an accountant before, you will find that most businesses have different situations for their financial needs. It may be very easy to replace the hamburger maker or the cook in the kitchen with a robot, but it is much more difficult to replace the person who can assess the situation. The challenge with artificial intelligence is that it doesn't have something that allows it to understand the context.

Whenever you go to pay your bills, you may not pay your bills on time on purpose. In an automated system, the bills will be paid on time every time. However, you may need to wait a week to pay a specific bill because of a certain reason. A lot of people delay paying bills because of reasons and one problem that robots have is understanding context, the reason why something is being done. This means that even though all jobs will eventually be replaced, the jobs that will be replaced last are the jobs that require context. You cannot automate the process of building a full-scale website, you can automate the design process, the building blocks, and many of the different elements of a full-scale website but that website changes based on the company needs.

Even the Creative Jobs

This means that eventually, even the creative jobs will be replaced once artificial intelligence machines can understand the context. Here's the problem though; why does it matter? Why does it matter that jobs will be replaced? Jobs exist to continue our survival and basically to give us something to do until we die. It's not really a bad thing if all the mandatory jobs are replaced by robots because there is always going to be something else to do. So you don't have to make hamburgers, but you can choose to create a shop of human-made food. That will become a specialty, shops that pride themselves on using only Human Services. Sure, you could automate a car fully, but a car is not going to speed down a runway at top speed to give you a drill thrill. Robots are designed to repeat routine tasks, things that you do for fun are things that only humans can do. Only humans can make human-made food or human-made clothing, something that will be seen as the new fashion style. The job market is always going to exist and there will always be something to do, you just have to have the right perspective.

What do you need to know to implement A.I.?

Easier Than Ever

The first thing to know and understand is that you are standing on the shoulders of giants. A lot of people don't like to start out with this because they might think it's a little arrogant, but if you are just getting into artificial intelligence, then you need to understand this. There has been a lot of work done in the past two decades regarding artificial intelligence, which means you are going to need to do a lot to get to where the frontier is at. That isn't to say that you can't do it within a reasonable time, it's just that you need to appreciate the complexity of this industry. Additionally, you need to understand that it has taken a lot of work to make things easy and while there are very easily implementable tools out on the market, understanding the core mechanics of how neural networks work is key to using these tools. The tools simply allow an individual to get the work they need to be done without having to deal with much hassle, understanding how those tools work is still something you're going to need.

Algebra to Calculus

The second thing that you're going to need to know is a variety of mathematical skills, depending on what you want your artificial intelligence to do. If you want your artificial intelligence to simply forecast the next week's stock prices, you'll mostly need to know statistics as well as maybe a little calculus. If, on the other hand, you want to utilize artificial intelligence to generate 3D pieces of Art then you may need some geospatial mathematics along with a little bit of discrete mathematics. There is a wide range of mathematical skills that may be required depending on what you want to do with it, but the reason why I specifically state algebra to calculus is that you will need to know algebra at least. Neural networks are designed with the understanding of the slope-intercept form as the most basic form of a neural node. It only gets much more complicated after that. Most of your learning will actually be solely mathematical and very little of it will be programming, but that is the third thing that you need to know.

Programming

You will need to understand programming to the degree of the tool that you plan to use. If you are going to a website that allows you to use a neural network that was already built beforehand, you're likely not going to need much programming. If you plan to utilize a localized version of a neural network, you are probably going to need to know how to program and access the graphics processor unit library that's compatible with your computer. A lot of people misunderstand this requirement because, in the beginning they are thinking about DirectX 11 or 12 or maybe Vulcan architecture, but these are graphical libraries. If you plan to create a localized neural network, you will need to know a significant bit about the hardware that you plan to use. This is because you can use the central processing unit or the graphical processing unit to do the job, but how you go about using it is definitely different.

Which jobs will be replaced the soonest?

Repetitive Tasks Are the First to Go

As I have mentioned several times at this point, the first jobs that are going to go are the ones that can be repeated. Flipping hamburgers, filing, writing checks, lifting things, stocking things, ensuring things are on shelves, and pretty much anything that requires a routine. That's almost all of the low-end jobs; the ones that teenagers and the elderly tend to find themselves at. These jobs will be the first to go because you don't need to pay wages to a robot and all you need to do is maintain the robot to extract the benefits. You will still need somebody in a managerial position to handle customers, but generally, all the basic jobs can be robots.

Now, it is important to understand that there will still be one person left to just be there. This is sort of like the individual that is there at the self-checkout. The individual is not really supposed to make sure that you are checked out and get all your groceries, they are there should anything go wrong. These jobs will become the new jobs that teenagers and elderly fit instead of the ones that require the person to check out. This means that Mom and Pop shops will probably still hire the person willing to look after the register during the business hours, but a company like Walmart or Target is likely going to hire one person to manage stocking robots.

There will also be an increase in the need for Maintenance Technicians and Maintenance Engineers, to ensure that the robots are properly maintained.

Jobs carried out via Rules Go Second

We've already begun seeing that jobs that require rules begin to have their own version of replacements installed. For instance, as I mentioned before there is now a contract lawyer artificial intelligence that would essentially replace lawyers that focused specifically on contract work. These positions primarily follow the rules and patterns, which means that even though it is significantly more difficult in routine than compared to stocking something on the shelf, it can still be automated given enough work.

Consultancy Goes Third

The last type of job that will go is a consultancy and the reason why I say this is because consultancy is a routine but contextual job. Sure, you could say that in consultancy, all you are doing is judging what can be added or subtracted from a workload so that the company makes more money. This is something that a machine can currently do, but the problem comes in the form of contextual understanding. You see, any machine can go and create optimization methods for a business, but the business has to create that machine to fit that business. This means that the business itself is providing the contextual understanding the business needs in order to make an effective evaluation of what is needed to optimize the business. When a person comes in to consult for a business, they need to understand the business before they begin suggesting anything. This necessity for a contextual understanding is something that can't be quantified by a machine just yet and so this is why that will be the last type of job to go. However, it will eventually go.

Which jobs are least likely to be replaced?

Inventors

The primary job that will not be replaced, I repeat it will not be replaced, is an inventor. An inventor is an individual who thinks outside of the box. They look at the market and they look at what available tools exist before they begin generating ideas for what can exist if you combine those tools. The reason why an inventor will not be replaced is that almost all companies require an inventor in order to begin a company in the first place. They are the thing that drives the industry. They absorb more data than any current processor or processor within the next decade would be able to sustain and abstract it into an invention. In other words, inventors don't have any rules beyond the rules of the universe. This means that you can't automate the job because there is nothing to automate.

Frontier Science

The next type of job that is not likely going to see any form of automation is Frontier science and this is primarily due to the fact that scientists want to keep machines away from science. That isn't to say that there won't be a lot of science that these machines are capable of and it isn't to say that these machines won't be helping to march forward in the frontier science, but machines are not likely to be the entity to march forward in the frontier science. There's too much mistrust of machines, there is too much paranoia around the singularity, and if we hand over science to the machines, then there will be nothing left for Humanity to do.

CHAPTER 7:

Self-Driving Cars and How They Will Change Traffic As We Know It

Aself-driving truck startup, Otto, sent one of its trucks on a 120-mile journey to deliver 51,000 cans of Budweiser. Uber, which has already vowed to eliminate human drivers from its workforce, bought Otto and is now experimenting with self-driving vehicles as a part of a marketing tactic that is meant to impress investors. Pay attention to the details of the journey to see the flaws of self-driving vehicles.

With an empty driver's seat, the driverless truck was surrounded by four police vehicles and three Otto vehicles that were meant to intervene in case someone got thirsty, or the truck broke down; two tow trucks were plowing through traffic ahead to ensure nobody messed with the truck's trajectory. The driver lounged in the back but took control once the truck left the highway. Otto later confirmed that they did the same route before with a human driver at the wheel who never had to take control. Budweiser logistics manager explained that they eagerly want to see this kind of delivery method scale. Shailen Bhatt, Colorado's Executive Director of the Department of Transportation, said that self-driving trucks are in a legal gray area, but the technology could, at some point, become as ubiquitous as automatic transmission. Neither Otto nor Budweiser manufacturer could elaborate on when they see self-driving trucks becoming a regular part of the traffic.

How many flaws did you spot? Driverless vehicles will need constant attention by humans, and in this case, a single car required attention from at least seven people (one driver per each vehicle surrounding it, not counting drivers in tow trucks) plus a driver in the back of the truck. So why is the driver there? Because the truck's sensors rely heavily on using immaculate highway traffic signs to navigate; once the truck is on dirt or gravel, the neural network driving it goes haywire.

Self-driving vehicles require an enormous infrastructure to work properly, and that is without humans interfering with it. It is quite likely human drivers encountering self-driving trucks would intentionally mess with it just for fun or to eke out a settlement, so there would again have to be a human driver in the cab just for optics. Companies that own and dispatch self-driving vehicles would then most likely push for human-free lanes, where neural networks have the right of way at all times and can form seamless convoys. How is that different from using a train to move cargo?

Further, self-driving vehicles are in a legally gray area, meaning they can't get insured or registered as regular vehicles can. It is unknown if self-driving trucks can scale, meaning we can sort of tell what happens if one self-driving truck is sent on a voyage but what happens if ten million are sent every which way at the same time? What kind of infrastructure would the logistics company need to build to manage that?

Plenty of things don't add up when it comes to self-driving trucks. Jumbo jets have had autopilot capability for some 40 years, but we still need a human pilot and a backup pilot, so self-driving trucks will, by all accounts, require more people to be hired. They obviously cost plenty of money and effort without an immediate return, so why are companies pushing for them? Without an apparent answer, the most likely reason is that there is a certain pride in being able to call one's own company fully automated.

Surveys done with potential self-driving car buyers showed that they overwhelmingly want a car that would destroy itself and its driver rather than kill the passers-by. The problem is, when they are asked if they would buy or drive that kind of car, they vehemently said, "No." The interests of tech giants to increase their reach and surveillance clash with societal norms, capabilities of neural networks, and even the human instinct for self-preservation stemming from the limbic system. Legal liability for this kind of thing would be enormous and no kind of suicide clauses in the purchase agreement would shield a tech giant from a flurry of lawsuits.

However, presenting the self-driving car as being operated by an AI that has been granted a status of deity could work as a legal loophole. There is already the precedent of "force majeure" or higher force that allows companies to slip out of contracts, most notably in cases where numerous property insurance payouts would bankrupt the company.

Force majeure is reserved for overwhelming events, such as riots and wars, but also includes elemental disasters, such as tornadoes and floods, that utterly destroy a certain area. Considered "an act of God," force majeure could be used after an AI has been presented as a deity, making it legally immune to lawsuits and contracts in cases of self-driving car pileups.

CHAPTER 8:

Robots and How They Will Change Our Lives

The field of AI has dramatically developed with many new general technological achievements.

Artificial intelligence (AI) is arguably the first exciting field in robotics. It is the foremost controversial. Everyone agrees that a robot would work well in an assembly line; however, there is not any agreement on whether or not a robot will ever be intelligent. Robots are software-driven machines that are sometimes capable of performing a series of actions autonomously or semi-autonomously.

Three vital factors represent a robot:

1. They are programmable.
2. They act with the physical world through actuators and sensors.
3. They are sometimes autonomous or semi-autonomous.

It is said that robots are "usually" autonomous as a result of some robots are not. Telerobots, as an example, is entirely controlled by a human operator; however, robotics continues to be classified as a subsection of AI. This representation can be one instance where the meaning of AI is not entirely clear.

It is tough to get specialists to agree precisely what makes up a robot. Some individuals maintain that a programmable machine should be able to "think" and make decisions. However, it is no standard definition of "robot thinking." Requiring a tool to "think" infers some level of AI is applied.

Robotics involves designing, programming, and building of actual robots. A minor component of it involves AI. Most AI programs are not applied to create or manage robots. Even once AI is employed to manage robots, machine learning algorithms are solely a section of the more extensive robotic system that additionally includes non-AI programming, actuators, and sensors.

AI involves some level of machine learning, but not always. An example is where innovative design is "trained" to retort to a selected input in a very sure means by use of far-famed inputs and outputs. The critical facet that differentiates AI from a lot of typical programming is the word "intelligence." Programs that do not involve AI merely perform an outlined sequence of directions. AI programs are built to mimic some degree of human intelligence.

Robots Features

Artificially intelligent robots are the link between AI and robotics. These are machines that are controlled by AI programs. Up until recently, most robots have been programmed to only perform a series of monotonous tasks. As earlier stated, dull monotonous activities do not need AI.

Robots need an energy supply, and several factors move into deciding what style of power provides the foremost freedom and capability for a robotic body. There are many different ways to get, transmit, and store energy. Generators, batteries, and fuel cells provide the power that is regionally kept, however more temporary, whereas tethering to an influence supply naturally curbs the device's independence and variety of functions.

The innovation that empowers automation sense has fostered our ability to speak to machines electronically for several years. Transmission mechanisms, like microphones and cameras, facilitate the transmission of sensory information to computers inside simulated nervous systems. A sense is helpful, if not essential, to robots' interaction with live, natural phenomena. As the human sensory system is attenuated into vision, hearing, touch, smell, and style- all have already or are in the process of being enforced into robotic technology somehow.

Featured applications of robots include:

- **Computer Vision**

One obvious application of AI to robots is in computer vision. Computer vision permits robots and drones to explore the physical world much more accurately. This is a technology of AI that the robots use to see. Computer vision plays an important role in the domains of safety, agriculture, health, biometrics, and entertainment.

Computer vision mechanically extracts, analyzes, and comprehends valuable data from one image or an array of pictures. This method involves the development of algorithms to achieve automatic visual understanding.

- **Unsupervised Machine Learning**

Robots are already utilized in manufacturing, however, typically in preprogrammed tasks. Robots may learn tasks with machine learning by being taught by humans or through unsupervised machine learning. While there is a concern that robots like these may replace individuals in industrial jobs, these robots may work alongside humans as "cobots", involving more collaboration with individuals rather than taking up their positions.

Some new robots even can learn in minimal capability. Learning robots acknowledge if a particular action (moving its legs in a specific manner, for instance) achieved the desired result (navigating obstacles). The mechanism stores this data and tries the productive action the subsequent time it encounters an identical scenario. Some robots will learn by mimicking human responses. In Japan, engineers have taught a robot to dance by demonstrating the moves themselves. Intelligence, deftness, sense, and power all converge to create self-governance, that successively may, on paper, cause a virtually personified individualization of mechanical bodies. Derived from its origin inside a piece of speculative fictional tale, the word "robot" has nearly universally observed by artificial means intelligent machinery with a certain degree of humanity to its style and thought (however distant). Therefore, robots are mechanically imbued with a way of individuality. It conjointly raises several potential queries on whether or not a machine will ever incredibly "awaken" and become aware, and by extension, treated as a person (or personal subject).

- **Human Error**

Another primary application of AI to robotics that has gotten attention in recent years is autonomous or self-driving cars. This sort of use is enticing because it promises to reduce human driver error that is the cause of most traffic accidents. A robotic automobile will not get tired, impaired, or inattentive while the human driver will. Even though there are several high-profile accidents involving autonomous vehicles, they show plenty of promise to be considered safer than human-driven cars. A significant area of analysis involving robots and AI is in medical technologies. Robots within the future might perform surgery without intervention from a doctor. Like autonomous vehicles, robotic surgeons might perform delicate operations for extended periods than human doctors will, while not feeling tired or making mistakes.

- **DEXTERITY**

Dexterity is the practicality of organs, limbs, and extremities, likewise because of the general varies of motor ability and physical capability of an animated body. In robotics, quickness is maximized wherever there is harmony between high-level programming and subtle hardware that comes with environmental sensing capability. Several alternative companies are achieving important milestones in robotic quickness and physical interactivity. This technology application lends an excellent deal of insight into the longer term of robot quickness. However, not all robots mimic the human physical type (those that do, are usually mentioned as "androids," whose Greek chronicle origin essentially interprets as "likeness to man").

Classification of Robots

The most popular robot classification includes immobile and mobile robots. These two types have completely different operating systems and thus have different capabilities. A majority of immobile robots are industrial robot operators who work in well-outlined environments tailored for programmable machines. Industrial robots perform specific and dull tasks such as bonding or painting elements in automotive manufacturing factories. With the development of human-robot interaction devices and sensors, robot operators are more and more used in a minimally controlled setting like surgery, which requires high precision.

In comparison, mobile robots maneuver around and carry out multiple tasks in considerably vast, ill-defined, and unforeseeable environments that do not seem to be designed explicitly for robots. These robots have to modify things that do not seem to be precisely renowned but which change over time. Environments like these will embody unpredictable entities like humans and animals. Some of the common mobile robots include robotic gutter cleaners and automated self-driving vehicles.

There lacks a clear distinction between the functions meted out by mobile robots and immobile robots. There exist three primary environments for which mobile robots would need considerably variable class principles as a result of the difference in the means of motion: terrestrial (for instance, cars), aquatic (for example, underwater expedition), and aerial (such as, drones). The classification is not strict; take, for instance, some amphibious robots that move on water and the ground. Robots that operate in these three terrains are further subdivided into pseudo groups: terrestrial robots either have legs or wheels, and aerial drones are light balloons or heavy craft, that are successively sub-grouped into fixed-wing and rotary-wing as in the case of helicopters.

Nowadays, robots do plenty of different tasks in several industries, and therefore the variety of jobs entrusted to robots is growing steadily.

Robots can also be grouped in accordance with the supposed application industry and the functions they perform as follows:

- Industrial robots that perform repetitive duties on manufacturing tasks are mentioned.

Industrial robots are robots employed in industrial manufacturing surroundings. Sometimes these are articulated arms developed explicitly for applications such as assembling, product handling, painting et al. If we tend to decide strictly by uses of this kind, we might additionally embrace some automatic guided vehicles and different robots. The first robots are said to have been industrial robots as a result of the well-defined surroundings simplified their style.

- Service robots, alternatively, assist humans in their tasks.

Domestic or social robots include several quite wholly different devices like robotic sweepers, vacuum cleaners, gutter cleaners, robotic pool cleaners, and various robots that may do completely different chores. To add, defense applications like intelligence activity drones and telepresence robots can be thought to be home robots if employed in that environment. Service robots do not constitute different varieties by usage. These can also be completely different information-gathering robots, robots created to indicate off technologies, robots used for analysis, etc.

Robots have also been increasingly used in the medical field, in surgeries, training, and rehabilitation. These are examples of applications that need sharper sensors and better user interaction. Medical robots are employed in drugs and medical establishments, the very first medical application being surgery robots.

- Military robots are employed in the military.

These kinds of robots include explosive diffusion robots, transportation robots, and intelligence activity drones. Usually, robots created at first for military functions will be employed in law enforcement, search and rescue efforts, and different connected fields.

- Entertainment robots used for recreation.

This is often an inclusive class. It starts with toy bots like 'Robosapien' or the running grandfather clock and culminates with real heavyweights like articulated robot arms used as movement simulators. Hobby robots are also in this class. They constitute those that you create for the sake of code. Line tracker robots, sumo-bots, are robots created only for fun and competition purposes.

- Space robots would come with robots used on the International Space Station.

Mars rovers and different robots employed in space exploration.

CHAPTER 9:

Artificial Intelligence Activities of
Big Technology Companies

The fact of the matter is that large technology companies are leading the way when it comes to the use of artificial intelligence. Indeed, many smaller companies have only explored the use of AI at their businesses because of the perception that they are losing ground to some of these other companies. The reality is, they are. In spite of long-established anti-trust laws, large companies are becoming larger than ever before, dominating their industries in ways not seen since the 19th century. In fact, these industry changes are happening so quickly that even the government has not been able to keep up, let alone small businesses that are looking to learn from big tech to stay competitive.

And that is exactly what these small businesses and their business leaders need to do: learn from big tech companies so that they too can make the most out of AI. What is so brilliant about the behavior of big tech when it comes to AI is that they not only create programs that use artificial intelligence to market to their customers, but they have their own AI teams that use AI to analyze company data and make business decisions. Indeed, the ability of AI to make business decisions is regarded as one of the trends in AI that is most likely to shape business in the future.

The most obvious applications of AI at big tech companies may be the products that these companies market that use artificial intelligence technology. Siri and Alexa are examples of artificial intelligence that millions, if not billions, of people use every day. Actually, these products have exploded onto the market so quickly that many people have begun using them without knowledge of some of the concerns that their use entails.

Big tech companies have been able to use AI so effectively, both in their businesses and in their products, because they have been at the forefront of AI research that has led to the development of new products. In fact, AI research is no longer sponsored primarily by governments, but by private industry, a picture of research that has essentially been in place for 30 years. Because these large companies are the sponsors of research in natural language processing (NLP) and artificial neural networks, they are usually the first to release products that make the most use of these technologies. In some cases, big tech companies acquire smaller companies that develop these technologies and incorporate them into their business.

Although, big tech companies will always have an advantage when it comes to being financially positioned to sponsor AI research, it does not mean that smaller companies cannot make their way in the AI world. For example, a smaller company might have an intelligent, close-knit staff that is capable of developing a niche AI that might be more difficult at a larger company that is being pulled in many different directions.

What this highlights here is the idea that money represents only one part of the ability of businesses to engage in AI efforts. Perhaps the most important aspect of the AI effort is brainpower. Large tech companies not only have the money to conduct AI research and invest in product development and marketing, but they are also able to attract teams of talented AI scientists and information scientists. These teams are essential to these companies being able to develop AI and use it to best benefits in their business.

When it comes to what small companies can learn from big company, one of the lessons, therefore, becomes that having a talented AI team is a way that a small company could potentially compete (or survive) against a larger one. Large companies have machine learning teams that are involved in developing AI technology and using existing AI technology better. If a smaller company is able to attract such a team, then they can see the same sorts of benefits that a larger company can. Smaller businesses can also be involved in creating products to market to customers, just as larger companies can.

Apple

Apple is one of the most innovative big tech companies around today. Apple realized early on the way that mobile devices were converging with the Internet of Things (IoT) to create great potential for business. The Apple iPhone has been the most successful mobile phone ever, and its popularity has shown no signs of slowing. Indeed, the popularity of Apple has allowed the company to leverage some of its other products, a few of which use AI.

Siri is perhaps the AI product that will be most familiar to people. Siri is a virtual assistant that serves as a component of iPhones, Apple Watches, iPads, and other Apple products. Siri uses natural language processing capabilities to understand language and complete tasks based on client requests. Siri truly represents the way that artificial intelligence software converges with IoT to potentially create an AI world. Actually, the fact that most devices nowadays have internet connectivity is what allows artificial intelligence to insinuate into the lives of modern-day people in ways that speculative fiction writers could never have imagined even 25 years ago.

Amazon

Amazon is, along with Google and Facebook, one of the so-called Big Four technology companies. Amazon has revolutionized not only the way companies use AI, but also the way companies market products, and the way companies do business. In many ways, Amazon represents the business of the future. With its wide range of products available for purchase and its use of IoT to allow customers to purchase and receive products, Amazon represents a commercial enterprise that few companies can realistically compete against.

But, Amazon really needs to be mentioned here in terms of its Alexa product. Alexa is another virtual assistant AI built with natural language ability. Alexa has been used with other Amazon products, include Amazon Echo, and it is able to aid customers in a wide range of activities, including setting alarms, obtaining information, and playing music. Alexa really represents what customers expect from commercially available AI products and the success that a company can obtain by understanding what customers want.

Let's face it; customers want convenience. We live in an information age and AI can work together with IoT to provide men and women with information based solely on voice-based queries. Alexa has improved over time to take advantage of the realities of AI technology to meet human needs (or rather, wants). Alexa has been integrated with a home automation system to allow users to control devices within their homes, including heating and cooling systems, alarms, and other devices. Smart homes represent another major trend in AI, and Alexa poises Amazon to be a part of this significant trend.

Microsoft

Microsoft is positioned to be a giant in artificial intelligence mainly because of the ubiquitous nature of its Windows operating system, and because of the massive amounts of data that it has access to. Microsoft is also the world's largest producer of software. Of all the companies mentioned on this list, Microsoft perhaps is the company that has been dealing with innovation and data management the longest. Also, because Windows is such an important component of computers, Microsoft is able to be a player in AI in ways that other companies perhaps cannot.

Microsoft uses AI in its business as a data management tool. It also markets AI to other large companies, like Carlsberg, the famous beer manufacturer. Microsoft AI technology is being used by Carlsberg to "fingerprint" beer, which allows the company to develop new beer varieties and predict taste. This allows Carlsberg to remain at the frontline of boutique brewing, allowing their business to stay competitive in an economic climate characterized by an increased number of players. In fact, Microsoft uses AI in ways that probably only they know about, allowing them to remain one of the most important players in data.

Google

Google is a big tech company that essentially came out of nowhere to dominate the internet. Google expanded from being a mere search engine to being arguably the world's most popular email provider and the most powerful (and popular) browser. This makes Google essentially into a Microsoft rival, as Google now has access to user information that may actually exceed that of Microsoft. Again, data is important as it not only allows companies to monitor their operations, but it provides training data for AI.

Google has a number of AI products that allow it to be a major player in artificial intelligence at big tech companies. It is at the forefront of natural language processing (NLP) capabilities of AI. These language abilities of AI are used by Google Translate AI and by Google Home speakers, which basically function as a type of virtual assistant responding to commands. Google also has AI products that it develops and tailors to business clients. Like the other companies on this list, Google has machine learning teams that allow it to come up with new applications for AI. Again, Google is able to do this because it has access to so much data, not just user information from searches and email, but data in the form of internet information pulled by its search engine.

What Smaller Companies Can Learn from AI Usage at Big Tech

There is a great deal that small companies can learn from how big technology companies use AI. Companies like Facebook, General Electric, and Tesla are also at the forefront of AI, either because of one particular type of product that is trending in importance (like self-driving cars at Tesla), or because their access to data allows them to experiment with AI in novel ways.

In fact, that is precisely the takeaway point about AI use at big tech companies. It is all about data. Companies like Microsoft and Google are so important in AI because data was not something peripheral to their business, but an essential component. This placed these companies in a position where they were unable to avoid data and its importance, positioning them to recognize early on how AI can be used to help them with data.

The days of ignoring data from company or equipment or customers are long in the past. Companies like Facebook and Apple do not ignore any of their data, and neither should you. Data provides insight to company leaders about changes they can do to make their business better, whether those recommendations come from AI or analysts within the company.

The first step that many companies can take, if they want to be like the big tech companies, is to figure out how they can place their data where it can be accessed and used by AI. This may mean scanning documents and placing them on a cloud, or investing in commercially available AI that is installed at your company and which is able to monitor different types of company data. Investing in AI as a small business is not as difficult as many business leaders think, and if you are concerned about the viability of your company, then it is in your interest to put some thought into how you can accomplish this.

CHAPTER 10:

Future of Artificial Intelligence

While the organizations make attempts to manage wide-ranging information and a growing range of gadgets, still quality decisions can be made on the basis of AI and the IoT due to a couple of new techniques.

In 2020, approximately 7.6 billion people will expectedly make up the world population. In the same year, the IoT connected devices are also expected to rise from 20 to 30 billion. In this scenario, how can Jane and hundreds of thousands of other people handle this too much information, how they can decide what is vital besides making the right decision in these circumstances?

If these gadgets and human resources are figured out, we can observe an exponential rise of data and this abundant information is already producing 'infoxication.'

Artificial intelligence, apparently, is one of the smart solutions to all of these challenges where certain tools are developed that have the potential to cope with information besides searching for reliable data sources. Moreover, informed decision making and improved cognition are other benefits.

Workplace hub generally focuses on the office, and particularly on the imminent workplaces. It makes use of a single centralized platform and combines all of an organization's technology. Also, this improves the productivity by curtailing the IoT related expenditure.

It delivers real-time insights through which business processes are transformed. With the acceptance of IoT and AI systems, the workplace hub will be transformed in the upcoming time to turn out to be a cognitive hub.

The intelligent edge computing and AI will be merged with this new technology. Besides, increasing the association between individuals and teams, human intelligence will ultimately be augmented to expand the network of human interfaces.

Within the digital sector, Cognitive Hub will serve a dynamic platform for information flows and it will offer augmented intelligence for masses at large.

Moreover, it will integrate future gadgets, such as: flexible screens, augmented reality glasses and smart-walls. For incorporating wisdom, Cognitive Hub will utilize AI to gather and process data with an aim to bring comfort for individuals, teams, and companies.

According to some people, cloud computing will vanish, but the fact is it will persist. Rather, it will diverge and become a cortex-like structure made of complex three-dimensional tree. Actually, cloud computing is a bond among cognitive computing, intelligent automation and other AI driven fields.

Huge work is yet to deliver in the cognitive hub; however, our working style has already been transformed by workplace hub and it enables us to control the growing intensification in information and gadgets.

Future of AI in 2020

Speaking of 'Millenials' and the generations to come, the modern-day discoveries do distinguish us from our ancestors. So far, human minds have invented simulations of almost everything. The brain was and it is the only common thing among us, our ancestors and the impending generation, which transforms our communication, thinking styles and working patterns. Researchers have predicted Artificial Intelligence for long. However, it was initially bonded with robots only.

Nowadays, AI has been integrated into almost everything in our use. AI is considered to be a software application which pretends to behave like humans.

It is a blessing in this modern day and age, since it has brought ease and comfort in the lives of humans, it facilitates us in early accomplish of tasks. In this way, minimum energies are consumed, time is saved and the work gets accomplished efficiently.

Programming

This has taken us to a new world of wonders, where things are taking place beyond our imaginations. AI provides us the connectivity and acts as continuity among discrete actions. We can say that you can interact with numerous things at one point in time, such as rapid conversion from one language to another. With the early introduction of computers, we have been following certain procedures for dealing with our actions, which can be customized from the settings menu. These rules are not required while transferring the same technology into AI. Rather, the algorithm is trained to associate with the course of actions.

Decisions

On the basis of the data extracted from management information systems, decisions today are made by the companies, since data is directly materialized from company operations, as a result of which, it is challenging to either make or break the rules. Decision making gets refined with the implementation of AI into the decision supporting tools. While defining customer data into predictive models, decision management technologies are also fostered by the proficiencies in AI.

On the basis of the major demographics, other departments, such as consumer and marketing are transforming their efforts because of this new trend.

In other words, it is a developed technology supported by digital banking, and, various enterprise applications are currently using this technology.

Interactions

With minimal effort, new forms of the interface are generated by the AI. The invention of mouse and keyboards has made us use these gadgets in our routine lives and we are still the users of keyboard and mouse. As far as digital communications are concerned, we have learned to design and develop the algorithms for benefits realization. We can observe a natural and smooth interaction, as the codes can now be transformed into human sentences and suspend the input from cameras and sensors.

What Should You Expect with Future of AI Technology?

Our actions, thoughts and living styles are being reshaped due to several technological innovations; however, the remarkable changes are delivered by the AI. While AI has recently penetrated the market, the AI has become flexible due to the modern revolutions. Evaluating its future, an individual can observe an environment where each aspect of our lives is controlled by AI.

Most Promising AI Innovations

Generally, our whole life will be reshaped through AI acceptance. While we are seeking AI driven tools at home, the corporations, businesses, and administrations are still using it.

The introduction of self-driving cars on the road is a big example. While this industry is expected to grow, regulations and policies to control AI-driven vehicles are being made by the U.S transport department. AI in the field of transportation aims to develop self-driving cars. Actually, AI has achieved the hallmark of designing the human-driven automatic cars and is expected to soon achieve self-driving cars with no human intervention.

To develop self-driving planes and buses, AI is still the major focus of many firms and the transport sector.

AI and Robotics will Integrate

AI has already been integrated with cybernetics, which is an ongoing progress. With the integration of AI technology into robotics, human beings will be able to improve their bodies with strength and endurance. While we may improve our bodies with the introduction of cybernetics, the disabled people could better realize its benefits. Life of the persons with amputated limbs or permanent paralysis can be improved.

AI will Create Complete Functional Robots

Nexus to above, we can build artificial life-forms as a result of AI technology. The knowledge of human-like robots capable of performing complex interactions has been extensively discovered by science fiction. Robots can have diverse significance as the field of robotics is being transformed with the presence of AI. For instance, robots can perform a risky task and take action, which otherwise may be unsafe for humans.

Impact on Humans

Gartner released some figures that 1.8 million jobs will be eradicated by the AI with the replacement of 2.3 million jobs by 2012. By observing this drive starting from earlier 3 industrial revolutions to this digital one, it is observed that there has been a considerable transformation in our lives and working styles and the same would continue in upcoming times. Take the example of a world, where people will work only two days a week. Such a time is soon expected.

However, AI is a big-big deal with these synthetic elements. Now, we live in realism because, in light of better learning, we are familiar with the rapid completion of task with maximum precision.

With automated reasoning as a positive glow in employment, 2020 will significantly witness the business advancement in AI.

The mark of almost 2 million net-new services is expected to be hit by AI based occupations till 2025.

A momentary employment misfortune has been associated with the different advancements; however, soon it is recovered by the benefits offered by these advancements. The business will change at that point, and this course will probably be taken by AI. The effectiveness of multiple occupations will be improved by the AI, doing away with several center and low-level positions.

Future of AI in the Workplace

AI and IoT are not only making our homes smart. Rather they are penetrating into a number of businesses besides interrupting the places of work. The efficiency, productivity, and accuracy within a company can be changed due to AI.

Nonetheless, many people are afraid of, due to AI progression, robots will replace the human workers and the same is perceived as a threat instead of a tool to transform ourselves.

With the continuing dialogues of AI back in 2018, it should be understood by the businesses that black-box potential and self-learning are not the solutions in this modern era. With the realization of AI based benefits to see value addition and to improve human intelligence, the unlimited power of AI is being experienced by many organizations.

Several decision-makers have begun using the capabilities of AI, because the advantages of intelligent systems are supported by significant evidences. According to a research work by EY, organizations integrating AI at the enterprise level see two main benefits: efficiency enhancement and informed decision making.

The competitive advantage is gained by the company which is the pioneer in implementing AI. Since it can curtail the recurring expenditures and may reduce other headcounts. This is a positive element in terms of business perspective, but people in different work places are likely to be taken over by machines, which is not an encouraging thing. Some conflict between machines and humans will obviously be created with the introduction of AI.

In the presence of innovative systems, our economy will greatly be affected by the AI with the creation of skillful jobs.

It is likely that AI will be emerged to replace certain jobs entailing iterative tasks and resultantly the current human ability will be concealed. The place of humans will be decided by the AI tools.

The tasks, such as: detecting corruption, loan approval and financial crime, will be executed by the automated decisions.

Owing to the development in automation, an enhancement in production levels will be witnessed by the organizations.

How to Maximize AI?

Since the AI progression will affect a number of jobs, it is also better to observe some of the problems that AI may take along.

By identifying an effective implementation, a solution to the bias problem around AI should be discovered by the business.

It must be ensured by the government that the profits of AI should be equally shared among the affected people and those unaffected by the developments.

The issues must be addressed at an informative level to successfully obtain the benefits of AI. The students can be empowered in AI related tasks as a result of educational systems.

Consequently, much importance is required to be given to STEM subjects. In addition, we should inspire subjects to enhance innovation and emotional abilities. Although, compared to humans, artificial intelligence will be productive, humans are always found efficient in performing better than machines and across jobs where relationship building and resourcefulness are needed.

The domain outside and inside the workplace will be transformed by artificial intelligence. Rather than emphasizing on the fear of automation, the technologies should be happily accepted by the businesses to ensure that the successful AI systems are going to be implemented for enhancing and supplementing the human intelligence.

Conclusion

Thank you for reading it to the end. Artificial intelligence and other applications of computers have fascinated men and women all over the world ever since knowledge about computers began to increase in the years after World War II. The human imagination has spawned ideas about the applications for computers that have led both to advancement in computer technology and fear that computers will one day replace us. In particular, artificial intelligence technology has been a source of fear because of the early days of AI, when this technology was associated with imbuing machines with human qualities.

But, intelligence does not have to mean "human" even though this implication is often present. It is interesting to ponder that images of artificially intelligent life in fiction almost always depict machines behaving in characteristically human ways: attacking human beings, being self-interested, being deceptive. If we separate cognitive or analytical intelligence from other types of intelligence, there is no reason to suppose that intelligence demonstrated by machines would necessarily lead to human-like behavior by machines.

There are many different ways to classify artificial intelligence with one major system focusing on those distinctions that we were just exploring. AI can be divided into analytical AI, human-like AI, and humanized AI. Human-like and humanized AI represents attempts by human beings to imbue AI with those types of bits of intelligence that are often thoughts of as the preserve of human beings (though this assertion in itself is debatable). Emotional and social intelligence are aspects of AI that can be programmed and which AI may eventually come to express naturally.

It goes without saying that there are ethical issues in artificial intelligence. There is, of course, the obvious ethical question of whether human beings should create creatures that are more intelligent and powerful than humans, but there are also questions of whether (as these beings become more "sentient") there is a need to protect the rights of machines that we have created. The issue of ethics in AI is usually divided into robot ethics – meaning the behavior that human beings exhibit relative to robots and the rights that robots may require– and machine ethics – meaning speculation about the behavior of machines as they become more intelligent and potentially independent.

No discussion of AI would be complete with an examination of deep learning and its applications. Deep learning potentially represents the future of AI as it leads to the creation of machines that have the potential to learn and adapt based on cues from their environment. Such machines are created with artificial neural networks that allow them to process information in the complex way that human beings do. With an understanding of deep learning, the reader became prepared to examine the applications of AI in fields like medicine and health and business.

Fictional portrayals of artificial intelligence may seem nonessential to the discussion, but they actually help us to get a picture of where AI is likely going to in the future. Just as computer scientists used theories espoused in science fiction literature to push the boundaries of computers and AI, so too can the AI researchers of the future find inspiration in the fiction of the past. What will artificial intelligence in the modern world look like? Well, if you believe films like Ridley Scott's Blade Runner then it will look just like us.

I hope you have learned something!